realizeone.

Common Ground

Developing a relationship with this Planet is essential for living a life of wellbeing. Beyond that, developing a relationship with this Planet can set the foundations for a meditative life.

Findlay McEwen

Common Ground

Findlay McEwen

Contents

Dedication

May this book light an internal spark that brings you closer to the Planet and yourself. May it provide you with a simple explanation of why the Planet is important, how we can make the most out of our time here and how to return to our hearts.

This book goes out to anyone with the openness to change themselves for the betterment of Humanity. This book goes out to those who wish to leave a lasting impact on this planet beyond their personal bank account, experiences or relationships. May you hear these words internally and may they shake out of you a drive to assist Humanity unfold into our collective highest potential. Most of all, this book is for those who wish to put the limited version of themselves to the side and bring forth a potent, absolute version of themselves.

Thank you to all who have allowed me to nurture the inner exploration which has allowed this book to spark itself into existence. Enjoy.

Introduction

This book looks to point out the obvious: by connecting with this Planet and resting in the limitless ocean of our hearts, we can begin to transcend the patterns of suffering we hold ourselves in. In the stainless abode of a conscious heart, one can begin to understand themselves in an absolute way. This book hopes to ignite an internal fire which will burn away any confusion which may be hindering your experience of life. Unfold yourself into the Common Ground of infinite intelligence by developing the stability of thought and emotion required to dive into it. This book looks to inspire that journey.

Over the past four years, I have been gifted with the opportunity to realign myself and move forward in a way which is fulfilling to me. With the help of patient parents, a supportive sister and helpful friends, I have been able to nurture my inner development in a tremendous way. Even when that list of supportive individuals doubted my plans or questioned the timeline, they provided me with the encouragement I needed to propel myself forward. Along with the book, we offer a 90-Day Program which is designed to help you experience the words in this book as a literal inner experience rather than simply an intellectual understanding. If, after reading this book, you would like to put these words into life-changing action, visit realizeone.org/call and book yourself a free strategy call.

I would like this book to serve as a reminder. A reminder that the Planet must come first in all that we do and a reminder of your true self. Beyond your body, mind and emotions, what are you? This book looks to release you from your limited identity and belief systems which have no real use to you beyond physical survival. Instead of spending a lifetime entrapped in your false identity, which is associated with the body and mind, you can begin to embody an absolute version of yourself with the help of this book. This book can be a map in itself to inspire a life-changing inner journey, however, these are mere words and to change your life requires action. I hope that this book provides you with a simple, yet clear outline of why we should connect with the Planet and how your heart can act as a doorway to the Ultimate because again, this book can act as a map to inspire your journey but you must chart out your route and begin your walk. So, enjoy what is written and use it as inspiration without accepting it as true or false, simply look within and see if the final answer awaits.

The Planet's Address

Dear children,

These bodies you are in,

Are but extensions of my own,

Extensions of your temporary home,

Enjoy this bounty but don't let it squander,

Everything you need is everything we are,

Enjoy the dancing of the wind through the stability of the trees,

Enjoy the tides of the water glistening beneath the nourishing sun,

Take breath with a smile and know that you are whole,

Connected to all you will never be alone,

Enjoy this impermanent position you have assumed,

But don't allow the movements to entangle you,

Love and abundance for all to see,

Love and abundance the new currency.

Homage to the First People

The collective dream was no more

The day we met them on that shore

The land is ours but they didn't listen

Their fear-filled hearts knew what they wanted

Our people stood no chance

Millions wiped away

Voices silenced and wisdom lost

But today is a new day

The future is bright and balance is a must

This land will return to its original plan

Love and Peace, for all to see

Love and Peace, the new currency

The Importance of Grounding

As you read through this book, you will come across various techniques which I have outlined to help you connect with the Planet while settling into your heart. As you attempt these methods, it is important to remain grounded. What does that mean? Remaining grounded means that you are present, alert and aware of yourself in your physical body. You are not straying off with thought and emotional patterns and becoming engrossed in your imagination. Here are a few things you can do when feeling ungrounded:

1. Get a bowl of soil and rub the soil in between your palms and on the soles of your feet.
2. Walk barefoot on the Planet.
3. Drink water.
4. Rub your hands togethers.
5. Press the insides of your palms.
6. Take a few conscious breaths in and out through your nose. As you breathe in, draw your naval in. As you breathe out, push your naval out.
7. Most importantly, remind yourself that you are safe, present and in full control of your mental and emotional process. You are simply observing it as it unfolds.

These are a few simple tips you can use to begin grounding yourself when you feel ungrounded. Of course, this is not medical advice and I recommend that you consult a healthcare professional before attempting any techniques outlined in this book.

Common Ground

Findlay McEwen

Chapter 1:

Benefits of Connecting with the Planet

Chapter 1:

Benefits of Connecting with the Planet

As I mentioned in the introduction, this book looks to point out the obvious: by connecting with this Planet and resting in the limitless ocean of our hearts, we can realize a Universal Common Ground. A Common Ground where there is no you or me, this or that, greater or lesser, friend or foe; simply an undisturbed ocean of blissful stillness. But how can we access it? I will look to outline that in this book. By redirecting your attention back to the Planet and then into your heart, you can begin to realize your true nature beyond your earthly existence. Let us begin with the Planet.

This Planet has offered us a gift unmatched. The opportunity to experience ourselves as individuals in these magnificent bodies is something which we seem to take for granted. These bodies are extensions of this Planet. Temporary tools for us to call home. We are only here for a short time and when we go, we must leave these bodies behind. So doing our best to enjoy our time while making use of it, is very important if we wish to leave behind a brighter tomorrow for the next generations. But how can we make use of our precious time on this Planet? How can we get the most out of this experience? It seems that these two questions underly most of our lives today: What is my purpose? Is there any meaning to all of this? These simple, yet profound questions circle around the same question: what are we? A question so simple, that it can stump the most educated minds. A question so simple, that it will make one return life after life to figure it out. Unfortunately for many, this is not a question that can be answered in words but rather realized through experience. I say *unfortunately* because it seems that most of humanity remains distracted by the physicality around them rather than the Infinite Intelligence within them. We can study physicality for millenniums but we will not arrive home. This body and the physical world we perceive through our five senses are not what we are. When someone falls dead, what is left? The body and everything attached to it. All the money you made, all of the relationships you formed and everything that you built physically is left behind. Now, I don't say this to strike fear into your heart, I say this to wake you up. These bodies, with such a limited life span, are being propelled into things which essentially mean nothing. Someone who focuses on finances can spend their whole lives building up wealth, only to leave it behind once they go. Yes, you may leave it to loved ones and set them up financially, but it no longer concerns you. Everything you spent your life working for drops off along with the body. This can be applied to most dead people. They spent their lives chasing or accumulating something which does not serve them after death. That's a bad investment if you ask me. I am only concerned with that which transcends death. Investing internally is the only investment you can take with you after you leave your body and connecting with the Planet is a great place to start.

How can we make the most of our time if everything drops off at the time of death? Great question. Developing a relationship with this Planet will ensure that your time spent on this Planet works for more than just you. If you spend your life working towards a physical goal, it will be left here along with your body. However, if you work for both a physical and internal goal, your work will transcend death.

Physically we want life to work in a certain way. Most of us at our core want life to be pleasant for everybody, wellbeing for all life on this Planet, so, there will always be meaningful physical work to be done. I am not saying that all physical work is meaningless; physical work done without the desire for an outcome can be a spiritual process in and of itself. However, it is useless to blindly run in one direction without considering where we're going. When we don't stop to ask ourselves why we are accumulating unlimited riches or why we must pursue pleasure, it will be a pointless pursuit. The benefits of our physical work can touch the lives of millions if we work in awareness and working with the Planet will allow us to develop this awareness. The awareness necessary to understand where the Planet is, what it needs and where it wants to go. As Humanity, the direction of the Planet is no different than our own. We may have developed our ideas of economy, education and religion, into functioning societies, but we must not forget reality. Reality is not within the physical world that we build up; it is within ourselves. Learning to invite the Planet into our internal reality for guidance can be helpful for all of us looking to build a meaningful life. So, working in a way that is guided by the internal reality will ensure that your work is not meaningless. I would like to make it clear that even if you do not enjoy your physical work or you don't see any meaning in it, you can still bring awareness into all that you do. This awareness is the fuel which you can use to continue developing internally, even if your physical work is not satisfying because again, the only real investment you can make, is an internal one.

Now with all that being said, how can we learn to receive this guidance from the Planet? This is something we will cover in Chapter 2. For now, let us focus on the why and not the how. As I mentioned, the direction of this Planet is no different from that of our bodies. These bodies have come from and will return to the soil, they are simply extensions of this Planet's body. So, understanding what direction the Planet wants to move in is crucial for a prosperous Humanity. For example, if ten cells in your body decided to ignore you and use up all your nutrients for their own imaginary plans you would most likely look to change that. Similarly, we as Humans have been running around on this Planet completely ignoring its needs. We use our resources as if they are unlimited without considering the consequences. We have even begun to look at pillaging space, just to keep up with our ridiculous plans. If we were invited into someone's home and they offered us a room to stay, most of us would be very grateful for that. We would clean up after ourselves and try not to overstay our welcome. We would not raid their fridge and use all their hot water; we would do our best to be good guests. It is no different than living on this Planet. We have been given temporary bodies to experience through, resources to use and land to live on. We have all the resources we need to live well on this Planet, but we need to have a conscious connection with the host to make sure we use our resources well. If we have a problem or are struggling with something, we should be able to contact the host for help. Connecting with the essence of this Planet is a great way to establish that line of communication. Much like texting your landlord or speaking with the host of the home you're staying in; we need to be able to tap into the Planet's core frequency to understand what it needs. This is something we can all begin to do individually and we will dive deeper into establishing this connection in Chapter 2.

As we have discussed, consciously connecting with the Planet can bring a Universal path forward for Humanity. However, there are plenty of benefits to be felt on an individual level as well. Our body, mind and emotions can benefit tremendously from a conscious connection with Nature. There is plenty of scientific evidence to confirm that grounding is very beneficial for the body. Connecting one's skin to the Planet is fundamental for balance. Mental and emotional balance both tie into the stability of the body and if the body is rooted in the Planet, through regular conscious connection, physical stability will follow. As the body becomes more stable and rooted in the Planet, naturally the mind and emotions will follow suit. In many ways, what we call our mind is simply the body processing information. What we take in through the five senses needs to be processed by the body and this processing of information doesn't exclude the memory our body naturally holds from our ancestry and memories. So generally, what we commonly refer to as our mind, is really just a replaying of our current memory load. Connecting with nature helps rebalance much of the memory you are dealing with and whether you are struggling with memories or future ideas, consciously connecting with this stable Planet will help bring stability to your current mental and emotional load. Opening your mental process to Nature will naturally bring balance. Moving your attention away from the replaying of memory and shifting it into nature, will bring you closer to that balance. Stepping back from the constant processing of memory is something made possible through a conscious connection with nature. Now, what do I mean when I say conscious? Simply observing. Not going into the forest and mentally rambling on but observing what is unfolding around you. I went on a walk through Mount Douglas the other day, a beautiful mountain in Victoria, BC, with plenty of forest on and around the mountain which you can walk through. As I walked, I came across an elderly man walking his dog. He took a moment to stop and mention how beautiful the forest is and of course, I agreed. He went on to tell me that his wife was out of town and it was now his responsibility to walk the dog, whereas normally he would go for a jog through the forest. He mentioned how much more he noticed and appreciated the forest because he was able to stop and look around. This is a great example of how much of a difference it can make when one makes the conscious effort to slow down and observe. This can of course be applied to any aspect of your life but for the purpose of this chapter, I will refer to nature. As you continue to make this effort to slow down and observe, even if in the beginning you spend your time mentally rambling, you will slowly become more and more stable within yourself. So, we can see that there are many benefits mentally, emotionally and physically when we take the time to connect with the Planet. Somewhat like a domino effect, as the body becomes rooted into the Planet, naturally the mind and emotions will also begin to follow suit.

As we begin to deepen our own connection with the Planet, we will have the opportunity to directly receive and transmit Planetary reverberations. Now what in the world do I mean by that? This Planet is a living entity as much as we are. We have our intentions for our own lives and this Planet has intentions for itself and us as well. However, the more engrossed we are in our own mental and emotional processes, the less clearly, we will be able to hear and receive the intention of the Planet. Humans must learn to cultivate this relationship with the Planet as it is clear to me and many others, that the Planet must be the dominant in this Human/Planet relationship. The Planet knows what it needs and, by extension, it knows what Humanity needs because we are the Planet. As we discussed, these bodies are nothing but extensions of this magnificent Planet. They are extensions of an intelligent force which already knows which direction it wants to head in. So how can we learn to listen to its intention and move accordingly? Well, that's the purpose of this book. This book is intended to turn our attention back to the one who gave these bodies form. The one who gave us the opportunity to experience ourselves as individuals living in these magnificent bodies. This book hopes to reunite us with the only force that can move us forward harmoniously, the Planet.

Unfortunately, for Humanity, many of us have resigned our fates to a Judgmental God living above the clouds. And because of this, many of us try to recreate what we consider to be God's will on the Planet. However, history has taught us that my God and your God never seem to agree on what Humanity needs. So, I say again, this Planet itself is the mighty equalizer, it is the one who knows how life on this Planet needs to be lived. This Planet knows itself completely and learning to tune into its frequency and translate that for Human understanding is a skill that we need in today's world. Setting up systems of education, where connection with the Planet is taught and emphasized will be extremely beneficial for all of Humanity. However, of course, that is a bit of a distant dream as I write this book. We must be able to begin nurturing that relationship now. We must begin the work individually and from there, a great societal shift will be made possible but the work must begin on an individual level.

What does it mean to listen to the planet? Imagining yourself listening to something that doesn't speak words must be rather difficult. We can replace the word listen with feel. Learning to feel the reverberation of the Planet within your body is all you need to do. When someone you love is upset, all you have to do is look at them to know how they're feeling. Many of us can simply look at someone we love and know what kind of mood they're in. This has come because of a deep connection you have with that person. You know them inside and out, you have become very familiar with their patterns so, you can understand them without hearing them. You simply have to see them and you will feel their current emotional state. Similarly, when we begin to deepen our relationship with the Planet and the five elements, we will be able to understand what they are expressing simply by paying attention. Shifting our attention to the Planet every day for a period of time is all you need to do to begin understanding and listening to the Planet.

It is our attention which will make all the difference for Humanity. What we focus on is what we will create. If we focus too much on the mental and emotional process of Humanity, we will find ourselves spiralling into a pit of doom and gloom. We can see it now. Turn on your TV or take a look at social media and you will see nothing but an emotional mangle. In one way or another, the majority of media today seems to rev up our emotional bodies which hold us in a certain state of unconscious repetition. Now, I don't say this to cause a revolt or anger within you, I say this to simply have you look at your attention span. Look at what you are investing yourself into and see if it can be improved. If we can shift our attention back to the Planet, back to the vehicle which has given and sustains this experience, then we will be able to shift Humanity into a brighter future. This is the fundamental idea that sparked this book into reality: turn your attention away from the mental and emotional pushing and pulling of physical life and turn it back into the Planet.

Findlay McEwen

Chapter 2:

How to Give the Planet a Voice

Chapter 2:

How to Give the Planet a Voice

So, how can we develop our relationship with the Planet to a point where we can understand what it is trying to express? I will use this chapter to outline three simple practices you can use to deepen your connection with the Planet. Before I jump into them, let me reiterate. The most important connection you can have with the Planet is a physical one. Internally, you can also deepen that relationship quite beautifully, which we will discuss in this chapter but essentially, as a Human incarnate on this Planet, you must take the opportunity to really dive deep and develop a relationship on a physical level. From there, an internal relationship will blossom beautifully.

As you take the time to consciously connect physically with the Planet, these practices which I will share can act as a great compliment to your physical connection. If you have already developed a meditation practice and have no issues sitting still, then you can jump forward to the first practice. However, if you find it difficult to sit still and sink into your practice try one of these two options:

Option 1:
1. Sit with your eyes closed and focus your eyes between the eyebrows.

2. Sit with your legs crossed or simply on a chair with your back straight and your right foot crossing over your left.
3. From there, place your hands on your knees with your palms facing upwards and your thumbs and index fingers touching or right over left in your lap.
4. Take a few deep breaths in and out through your nose. As you breathe in, pull your navel (belly button) in as well. As you breathe out, push your navel out.
5. Repeat this cycle of breath seven times.

Option 2:

1. Sit with your eyes closed and focus your eyes between the eyebrows.
2. Sit with your legs crossed or simply on a chair with your back straight and your right foot crossing over your left.
3. From there, place your hands on your knees with your palms facing upwards and your thumbs and index fingers touching or right over left in your lap.
4. Inhale once through your nose and extend your exhale through your nose. Make sure that your exhale is longer than your inhale, I like to make it three times longer than the inhale.
5. Feel your heart and abdomen empty out and hold that feeling of relaxation for as long as you're comfortable.
6. Then take another deep breath in and repeat this until you feel a deep sense of relaxation.

Practice 1: **Connecting with the Essence**

1. Now that we have settled into our practice we can begin with the mediation. Sit with your eyes closed and focus your eyes between the eyebrows.
2. Sit with your legs crossed if you can, with the right leg resting over your left leg. If you can't do that, simply sit with your legs crossed or on a chair with

your back straight and your right foot crossing over your left.

3. From there, place your hands on your knees with your palms facing upwards and your thumbs and index fingers touching.
4. Continue to breathe in and out through the nose in a way that feels comfortable for you.
5. Slowly, gently become aware of your heart. Notice how it is beating and how that relates to your breath. Don't try to control or fix anything. Simply notice. Notice how your breath is moving and how your heart is beating.
6. Once you have deepened this awareness, begin to envision the Planet in your heart space. Visualize the Planet in any way you feel comfortable. You can imagine a tree, a body of water or the entire Planet spinning in your heart. However you do it, simply bring the essence of the planet into your heart space.
7. Continue to breathe through your nose and remain aware of your heart.
8. Continue this practice for 5 minutes.

The purpose of this practice is to connect with the core essence of this Planet. By using the power of imagination and visualization, you are calling and inviting the essence of the Planet into your mental framework. The more you practice this, the deeper it will become. The more aware you will become of the Planet and its own essence. From there you will begin to understand the Planet intuitively. Just like looking at someone you love, you can understand how they're feeling by simply paying attention. Developing a relationship with anything, whether it be the Planet, a person or an animal, requires attention. Simply paying attention without hoping for anything in return: that is what these practices are meant to establish.

Practice 2: **Mixing Intentions**

This Planet we are on has an intention of its own. It has its own journey which it is experiencing as it travels through this Universe. Similarly, we too, have our own individual intentions which we have come to this Planet with. Unfortunately, for most of us, we don't know what our true intentions are. We are too distracted by physical pursuits to sincerely turn inward and uncover our own intentions. This practice is a great way of bringing forward your own authentic intention and aligning it with the intention of the Planet. But how? Simple!

1. Stand with your feet shoulder-width apart.
2. Rest your arms down by your sides and close your eyes.
3. Focus your eyes between the eyebrows and begin to breathe in and out through your nose.
4. Similar to the first practice, begin to settle your awareness down into your heart. Take a few breaths to allow yourself to settle into the practice.
5. Once you feel that you have begun to settle and your breath has become slowed and subtle, imagine this: on one full cycle of breath imagine that a green light is flowing up from the core of the Planet through the soles of your feet to the top of your head.
6. On your next cycle of breath, imagine that a golden light is flowing down from the Cosmos into the top of your head and down to the soles of your feet.
7. Continue these cycles five times, starting and ending with the green light from the core of the Planet.
8. On your final exhale, imagine that you are breathing out all green and golden light through the soles of your feet.

The purpose of this visualization exercise is to help you open up to the intention of this Planet and the Universal intention you have come to fulfill while you're in this Human body. This is a simple way to allow both intentions to mix and mingle with one another, ensuring that they become clear and grounded within the cells of your body. Also, aligning your intention with that of the Planet will only assist in bringing forward your dream into reality. Much like anything, it takes time and practice to learn to become familiar with the subtle force of intention that this Planet and your life are running upon. We tend to hear the most in the sound of silence. So, listen closely to the stillness of your heart after completing any of the practices outlined in this book.

Practice 3: **White Tunnel of Light**

For the final practice, I will outline a simple way for us to connect with this Planet. Whether you meditate or not, this is possible to do for all of us. It requires an open mind and an open heart. This can be done with a tree, a body of water, the sun, etc. but for the purposes of this book, I will focus on a tree.

1. Go outside and sit in a park, walk through the forest or simply sit at a bus stop with a view of a tree. Just make sure a tree is in your line of vision.
2. Now, with your eyes open bring some awareness into your heart. Similar to the first practice. Just become aware of it as you begin to breathe in and out through your nose.
3. Once you begin to focus, move your focus to the tree and open to it in gratitude. Simply say, "Thank you tree" within your heart.
4. Now imagine a white tunnel of light emanating from the core of your heart, connecting you and that tree.
5. Continue to imagine this tunnel of light for 30-90 seconds and feel that connection of gratitude build within your heart.
6. After a sufficient amount of time has passed and you feel that you have opened in gratitude to that tree, simply sit silently in the awareness of your heart.

This is a simple way to develop the necessary connection needed to begin listening to the Planet's needs. It is a great way to use visualization to open up your own mental framework to include that tree's framework. By doing this, you are opening yourself up to the planet in a phenomenal way. Now I know that visualization is not for everybody and some may see it as nonsense but you may give this a try and notice something. Try it a few times and see. Much like a scientist dissecting a body who simply wants to know the truth; they're not interested in right or wrong or their own beliefs, they simply look. That's what I am asking of you with this book and these exercises, simply look. Don't sit in the stagnant pool of your beliefs. Look for yourself and see if you notice anything at all. If, however, you are afraid of the prospect of looking like a lunatic in front of others while staring at a tree and imagining a white tunnel of light emanating from your heart, don't worry, you can do this practice silently within yourself and no one will be the wiser.

These practices are simple ways to become familiar with the core reverberation of the Planet itself while allowing you to become open and receptive to it. With these three practices, I may have stretched what you consider real or not. You may think that visualization is pointless and not 'real' but let us take a moment to think of what it means for something to be 'real'. Imagine you had never seen or heard of a Zebra before. You only knew of the animals which lived in your neck of the woods and refused to acknowledge anything else as real. Next thing you know, you fly to Zambia, in southern Africa, and you see a majestic Zebra prancing about. Prior to that trip, you may have dismissed that Zebra as a work of fiction but now, with physical proof, you can acknowledge its existence. Similarly, if one of these practices seems ridiculous to you, I am saying that you can have the proof for yourself, you can see the Zebra yourself. You don't need to limit yourself to what you think is real or what you think you know. There is an ocean of limitless possibilities in the heart of every conscious being. One of these possibilities includes visualization. Visualization is a way of aligning yourself with a frequency you desire to align with. In this alignment, you can learn, expand and grow. Using visualization and nature is a great way of learning, expanding and growing in alignment with this Planet. If you think it's ridiculous, that's great, I am giving you the plane ticket to go check it out for yourself.

Common Ground

Chapter 3:

Social Integration

Chapter 3:

Social Integration

If the first two chapters stretched your ideas of what's real and what's not, I hope this chapter stretches your ideas of what's possible and what's not. I would like to explain how simple it is for one person to make a sincere dent in the social makeup. Simply by learning to live in a way which reflects our core principles, we can begin to shift the collective in a direction which is beneficial for all. I will explain my views on society, what it takes to make a change and how we can uncover and live by our own core principles. Let us begin with society.

See, what is society? Society is just an idea which has a strong hold over large groups of people. It is commonly seen as the borders within which people live. If you step outside of the borders, you may be deemed crazy but on the flip side of that, if you step outside of them, you may also feel a sense of absolute freedom. The idea of society has kept people in order. It has kept us believing that there is a greater power which can decide the fates of our lives. This power is normally seen as the government. The government can decide what we do and do not do. This power can also be seen as the economy, dominant religion or education system. Regardless, the principle remains the same: the vast majority of societies in the West today, operate off of the assumption that there is a greater power outside of me which has my best interest in mind. This belief has kept our societies in order over the years. Traditionally, the kings and queens of Europe were always seen as the more intelligent and competent of us all, that's why they sat at the top but of course, that is not the case. So, for the remainder of this chapter, I ask you to forget about the concept of society as you know it. Rather, look at it as a larger version of yourself because after all, society is just a large group of people. So, imagine that it is just a large group of *you's*. How would you like this world to look if you could impart your will on it? How would you employ our limited resources? Take some time and think about that. In the meantime, I will give some ideas of my own and a simple three-step framework you can use yourself to figure out what you want.

As I mentioned, our idea of society is just a label for a group of people living and working within the same area. This is nonsense. Each human has their own ideas, intention and free will to operate how they wish. Our very bodies have multiple 'societies' of cells working together towards the preservation of our bodies. So, to classify a group of individual humans with free will under the banner of a particular society is making the assumption that we all are working towards the same goal. If that were true, what are we all working towards? Where are we headed? If you sincerely ponder those questions, you have begun to shift the greater society. However, with all that being said, it can be very daunting to step outside of the societal lines when that is all that you have known. It can be hard to stray away from the footprints your parents, grandparents and great-grandparents have followed. That's why I have decided to go ahead and write this chapter. Let it serve as a spark of inspiration for you to live a life of absolute freedom without the imaginary confines of society. If we wish to shift society in the direction of consciousness, we must first take the steps within ourselves to see that unfold. If you wanted to fix your computer, hopefully, you would take it to someone who has done it before. Someone who knows how to fix it and embodies the knowledge of fixing computers. Similarly, for us to shift our societies we must first embody and put into practice the core principles we wish to see on a larger scale. It really is that simple.

Society is like a wall of bricks where each human is one brick on that wall. All it takes is one brick to change its color for another brick to change its color and another and another. That's a nonsensical example but it illustrates how easy it can be for one person to make a difference. When we have a group of people blindly walking towards the same destination, all it takes is one person veering off in their own direction to cause others to begin thinking for themselves. There are many examples from history of individuals breaking the norm, which leads to greater evolution for Humanity. Noam Chomsky and Desmond Tutu are two prime examples of how true individuality can shift an entire social makeup. Individual thinking, even in one moment, can alter the societal patterns which most of us unconsciously operate within. That's what this chapter is for, that's what this book is for and in many ways, that is what my life is for. Simply wake up and ask yourself where you're headed. Why am I confined to a life blueprint which millions before me have done? Why can't I change that? You can. Change yourself and just watch how the people, circumstances and opportunities around you change as well. It just takes genuine change on your part. Authentic embodiment of your core principles is all it takes.

Let me share a simple three-step framework for you to use to help you begin embodying and understanding your own core principles. It is important to remember that it requires consistency to realize authentic change and this framework is no different. I ask that you give it a try for seven days and just see if you notice a difference. Make a chart in a notebook, on your phone or computer, but keep track of your progress for seven days and see if you notice a difference.

Core Principles: Three-Step Framework

1. Sit with your back straight and eyes closed, with your eyes focused between your eyebrows. Begin to breathe in and out through your nose. As your breath becomes more subtle and slow, gently bring your awareness into your heart space. Just notice how it feels and how your heart is moving. Don't try to change it or alter it, just observe it. While continuing to breathe in and out through the nose, with the eyes focused between the eyebrows. Do this every day for 15 minutes in the morning.

2. Once you begin to feel that sense of ease envelop your chest and upper back, ask yourself "What feeling do I want my future to embody?". Simply allow that question to hang in the air and see what you feel. Do your best not to force a feeling or hang on to what you think you want. Don't imagine an answer, simply look. Simply allow life to show you how a beautiful future feels like for you. You will begin to align yourself with that reverberation by continuing the practice.

3. Spend 15 minutes a day in a forest, by a river, in a park, connecting with the five elements consciously. Simply by being outside and being aware of the natural movement of this Planet.

As you continue to practice this framework, you will begin to move towards your core principles and you will begin to embody the change you wish to see. You will begin to embody the intention you have come to this Planet with, because again, simply living from your core intention is all you need to do to begin shifting society in the direction of evolution rather than disintegration. It is only because we haven't stopped to ask ourselves where we are headed or why we believe in what we do, that we have found ourselves in such a difficult situation for Humanity. Taking a moment to stop and reflect on what intention we are holding as we move into the future, is all we need to do to begin crafting a brighter future for all. Beyond that, evaluating the individual identity which we hold and the emotional response that comes along with that is something we all need to do. In the next two chapters, we will discuss how we can begin to work with the Planet to go beyond our limiting identity which causes us so much suffering. We will then discuss how we can use the Planet and its elements to go beyond the confines of our emotions.

This chapter has been my attempt to stretch your idea of what society is. To help you see that society is just an idea placed over a collective group of people. However, you are under no obligation to confine yourself to that idea. Instead, you can begin to embody the core principles which you hold as true and begin to craft a life which can shift society into a more inclusive, loving and accepting place. Because even though society is just an idea, it is an idea that many people have accepted as reality thus solidifying it. So, shifting that pattern we know as society, takes individual thinking and courage. Follow the three-step framework outlined above and you will begin to think for yourself while developing the courage you need to act on your core principles.

I have mentioned the phrase 'core principles' multiple times already in this book. For those of you wondering what that means exactly, consider it as the ideal dream *feeling* you want the world to embody. When we strip away the desires for money, sex, food, conquest, etc. and sit in the core of our hearts, what does an ideal future feel like? Words like compassionate, inclusive, joyous and freedom may come to mind. As these words become clearer within yourself, you will begin to embody them in every action you put forward. Again, it may seem like it won't do much but all it takes is one person to stand up and act kindly, for another to follow suit. It just takes one person to think for themselves for another to do the same and another after that. Wake up, look around and feel what you want in a dream future for yourself and Humanity, then begin to align yourself with that feeling through your everyday actions: this is all it takes.

Findlay McEwen

Chapter 4:

Expanding Identity

Chapter 4:

Expanding Identity

Who are you? What are you? I posed this question at the beginning of the book. A seemingly simple, yet profound question that will stump the most educated of minds. It seems to me, that the chief reason for our suffering is our false identity. Our unshakable claim that we are this body and everything that comes with it has caused a raft of suffering throughout Humanity's time on this Planet. To think you are something impermanent is the greatest error we have made. Waking up in this body and claiming it to be yourself is no different than waking up in a car and claiming it to be you. Say you woke up in a car and looked around and all you could see, for miles on end, were other people sitting in their cars mistaking it for themselves. You would be forgiven for making the same mistake yourself but you would not be forgiven if you did not investigate. If you did not roll down the window or attempt to open the door. If you just sat in it and accepted its comfort as the Ultimate, you would never know the freedom of being able to walk around and use your two legs. You would waste a life by accepting your circumstances as normal, instead of looking for something beyond that. Most of us look to enhance our lives by enhancing our physical life. Using the car example, if you woke up in a rust bucket of a car, you may look to upgrade to a newer, faster model. Similarly, to human life, we think that upgrading our houses, bodies, relationships, etc. will enhance our lives, yet we still remain clueless as to what we are. We enhance the physical surroundings while remaining hollo within, without a drop of awareness invested internally, we go on chasing and accumulating temporary physical objects. The physical may give us a certain degree of comfort but it will not give us what we need to know ourselves. It will only solidify the boundaries of our identity while keeping our gaze fixed externally, continually ignoring our internal wealth. So, what are we? Don't ask me, find out for yourself. This chapter is for those who are sincere in their quest to settle into their true nature. This chapter is for those who want to propel themselves out of the cycles they have been living in and into an inner wealth which has remained untouched for most. This is for those who dare to open that car door.

Now, to be clear, I will not take you to that state through words but I can help you clear the road. I can help you set up your internal world for deeper insight and the first thing we must consider is our identity. What is it? Why have I claimed it? And how can I go beyond it? Expanding our identity beyond the confines of this body can begin with the Planet. Think of your body, where has it come from? What is it made out of? The Planet. It is an extension of the Planet itself and because of this, we can begin to identify with the Planet. In the same way, we identify with our family, nation, favourite sports team, race etc. we can identify with the Planet. We can make the Planet a part of who we are. To do this, go outside and simply thank the Planet for this experience you are having. Thank the Planet for your body as if it were your maternal mother. In that way, we can begin to expand the borders of our identity beyond the confines of this body. We can use the emotion of gratitude to transcend the borders of our limited identity. For example, when you fall in love with a sports team and take them on as a part of your identity, you are expanding the borders of your identity through emotion.

Think about a team or group of people that you love. You only identify with them because of your emotion attached to them. When something happens to them, good or bad, you are now affected by it. So, in the same way, we can begin to take on the Planet as a part of our identity to begin expanding beyond what we thought we were. Now, of course, there is still plenty of work to be done to demolish the borders of your identity but this is a great place to start. As we move through the book, I will hand you tools to use to begin expanding and dissolving your current limited identity.

Identity is just a word, which you may be getting tired of reading by now. However, when it comes to envisioning our identity, we can see that it is just a group of labels which are circling around the 'I' thought, attached to that 'I' thought through various emotions. For example, you popped up in your body. Now you claim to be an 'I' in that body. You claim to be a permanent individual but you are not. Let us use the car example again, here you are in a car claiming to be it. You then begin to identify with the colour, shape, size, make, model and year of the car. You limit yourself to the descriptions of that car because that is what you think you are and because of this, you now fall into larger groups of people who identify with the same features of your car. This is the same nonsense Humanity finds itself in. We jump into groups of people who share our race, religion, nationality, sexuality, age, etc. because we think that's what we are. Yet, we are something far more profound than that. Just imagine, you only hung out with people who had the same car as you. I'm sure you would make a few friends but after time you would want to expand beyond that. We have entire generations of countries fighting against one another simply because I stand on this side of a line and you stand on that side. We have divided the Planet and caused emotional rifts which continue to claim millions of lives and this all goes back to the false sense of 'I' which we all seem to cling to. I am this and you are that: that is delusion. Go into a forest and draw a line on the ground. Declare that everything on the left side of the line is one country with a strict belief system, then tell the right side that they are an enemy country with opposing beliefs. Next, go to work and tell your boss about your new project. Become emotionally attached to that line in the ground and do your best to convince them of its relevance to their lives. Imagine how you would be looked at by other people if you went about this with absolute involvement. You would probably lose your job and many friends, but that's what all of Humanity has done. Drawn lines in the sand and claimed ideas associated with that land. This is one big dilemma we find ourselves in. I say all this not to dampen the real impact these lines have caused and all of the suffering which has followed; I say this to have you evaluate the origins of your own identity and why you're so wrapped up in it.

If we wish to go beyond these borders of our identity, we can utilize the Planet to help facilitate that expansion. As I mentioned, simply going outside in sincere gratitude is a great place to start, using your emotion to expand your borders of identity is a very real possibility. However, you can take that further by beginning to observe nature itself. Watch as a leaf falls to the ground and eventually merges with the soil, notice how a raindrop disappears into a river, see how a fallen-over tree becomes a fertile ground for plants to blossom. Nature is in constant flux. No concerns with you vs me or right and wrong. Simply life without the chokehold of identity.

A human without the chokehold of identity can become a boon for Humanity. They can shift the consciousness of an entire nation; they can write a book or propel a spiritual movement; they can do whatever they need to do to wake people up beyond the confines of their identity. I mentioned above, that a simple way we can begin to go beyond identity is by opening in gratitude to the Planet and by simply observing the natural world. We can take this one step further by investigating our hearts. I will outline one simple exercise which I have already mentioned in earlier chapters, that can help us step back from the labels which we cling to. This practice is a great way to begin settling yourself down and detaching from the movement that you seem to be clinging to. By learning to settle our hearts, we can begin to step back from the endless movement of the mind and emotions and we can begin to let go of the identity which continues to uphold our suffering, yet we refuse to give up. I would like you to approach this practice with the discernment of a scientist who simply wants to know the truth. Do your best to place your emotional attachment to the labels you call your identity to the side. When you take a moment to consider what you think you are, all it is, is movement. Science will tell you that all physical life is movement. Frequencies reverberating at different pitches; this includes our bodies, thoughts and emotions. So, knowing this, we can begin to accept that everything we claim to be is simply movement. The nation you stand on, the body you stand in, the name you carry, the family you hold and even the emotions you feel are all frequencies. It is all movement. This leaves us with stillness. That is something I want you to experience with this exercise. Try this:

1. Sit with your back straight – either in a chair or on the floor cross-legged. Close your eyes and focus them between the eyebrows. Hold this for the entire length of the practice.
2. Begin to breathe in and out through your nose.
3. As your breath becomes slowed and subtle, move your awareness into your heart space. Just notice how it feels.
4. Simply sit in that space of awareness, noticing how your heart feels.
5. As it settles down, on your next inhale repeat silently in your heart, "I am Universal". Then

take an extended exhale which you feel completely empties your chest and abdomen.

6. Hold that space of silent awareness, noticing how your heart space feels. Continuing to breathe in and out through the nose with your eyes focused between the eyebrows.

7. After observing this space of stillness, open your eyes slowly, rub your hands together and drink some water if needed.

Continue this practice for seven days and see what you notice. For those of you who truly want to transform your lives, practice this every day for 21 days. The length of this practice is completely up to you, see how you feel when doing the exercise and decide how long you wish to hold it for. You can practice it for anywhere between 30 seconds to 30 minutes. This is a simple yet profound exercise for you to begin transcending the borders of your identity. You can begin to identify with the spacious stillness in your heart instead of the entangling labels in your mind. As you practice this with sincere intention, you will begin to notice how difficult it can be to step back from the entangling emotions which are holding you to your identity. The next chapter is about understanding our emotions and seeing them for what they are; from there we should be able to step back from them and free ourselves from their entangling hold.

Findlay McEwen

Chapter 5:

Observing Emotions

Chapter 5:

Observing Emotions

You may find that as you begin to evaluate the borders of your identity, you can't seem to create that inner distance between yourself and the identity: this is emotion. Your emotions are so intensified by your identity that it makes it impossible for you to see things clearly. You try to look over the wall of your identity but your attachment to the comfort of the side you're on makes it difficult to step outside of those walls. It's like you're in the car and try to open the door but it is terrifying to step out when everyone else just stays within the comfort of the car. All you've known is the comfort of your car so it can be difficult to step outside of that. Your identity has become so comfortable for you, it has become the armour that you show off to the world to feel like you belong, to feel like you are something. So, as soon as something or someone makes you go beyond that sense of comfort, it is very natural to retreat back into the patterns of thinking which feel familiar. But I don't care for that. I couldn't care less if you are comfortable or uncomfortable. Remember, to truly see your own self you must have the discernment of a scientist who wants to know truth. A scientist who cuts into a frog is not concerned about their own emotions, they simply push that to the side and find what they're looking for. I am asking the same of you as you push aside your identity and look to go beyond those limitations. It may be difficult at first because your emotions are so entangled in the idea of who you are, that as you begin to transcend that idea your instinct may be to fall back into that comfort zone which does not challenge those emotions. But again, I am not looking to comfort you or leave you unchallenged, I want you to go beyond the limitations you have imposed on yourself.

If we are to think of our identity as the walls we are confined in, our emotions are like the chains holding us trapped within those walls. Little did we know we had the key to unlock those chains and walk out of those walls; the key is in your heart. The key to absolute freedom from suffering is in the stillness within your heart. With that being said, it takes sincere work to go beyond these limitations. There must be a burning desire to go beyond the suffering you have become accustomed to. If you would like to sincerely work to transcend this suffering, head over to realizeone.org/call and book yourself a free strategy call to learn more about our 90-Day Program designed to do just that. And if you find that the desire to transcend your suffering is not burning within, this book is a spark to light that fire within you.

I'm sure most of us know the feeling of intense emotions. Whether they are positive or negative, they can entangle us before we are even aware of them. We don't have to be aware of why we are feeling the way we are, we just begin to move in that direction unconsciously. So, our work is to become conscious of the emotions we energize on a daily basis. Take a moment to think of your daily life; what emotions pull you forward throughout your day? What do you go about doing and what feeling are you hoping to get from those activities? Sit for a moment and think about it. Really, why do you get up in the morning, what work do you go about doing and why do you do it? What feeling are you hoping you achieve by doing your daily work? Simply evaluating this can help us begin to identify the emotions which blindly rule our lives. For us to stand back from our identities it takes awareness of our emotions. Again, it's not always that easy, so beginning by simply evaluating the current emotional patterns we are in, can help us create that space. If you're still finding it difficult to create that inner space between you and your emotions, try this three times a day:

1. Take a deep breath in and out through your nose and drop your awareness into your heart.
2. For 30 seconds become aware of how you feel, what is unfolding around you and what has triggered you to feel that way.
3. Do your best to come back to that place of natural ease within your heart and begin to notice how you get pulled out of that ease as emotions arise.

Doing this simple exercise three times a day can give you the awareness you need to begin identifying what triggers different emotions within you and how you can begin to remain untouched by them. In the previous chapter, I outlined a simple practice which can help you settle your heart and come to that place of ease. If you continue that practice you will be able to blend it with the exercise I just mentioned and you will begin to notice the difference between you and your emotions. You will begin to notice how you feel when your heart is settled and at ease, versus how you feel when your emotions are pulling you around. That is all we need to do to begin settling in our hearts and becoming aware of that ever-present stillness within. Our identities and the emotions which follow are like waves on the ocean; they may rise and fall but you remain untouched. In the stillness of your heart, you remain untouched. Again, it takes sincere work for one to become free from their self-imposed limitations but it is possible for anyone who truly yearns for that freedom.

As you become more familiar with the stillness of your heart, you will notice how your emotions act as a magnetic movement drawing you outward into physical engagement. As a thought arises out of that stillness, your emotion energizes it and naturally you follow that with words, thoughts and actions. The purpose of settling your heart is to have you become familiar with the immense freedom of the inner stillness which pervades all thoughts, emotions and actions. Think back to a time when you experienced awkward silence. What was awkward about that situation? It was simply your thoughts. Your uncontrolled thoughts which you energized with an emotion of awkwardness caused you to feel like that silence was awkward. But that silence was just silence. Innocent and pure. You sullied it with your own thought process and labelled it based on your own emotions. The same is happening in day-to-day life. We are sullying the beautiful, blissful silence with our mental and emotional rambling. In silence, the warring nations are equal and the poor are no different than the rich. However, in the noise of thought, emotion and physical action, we create borders, identities and destruction out of pure confusion. Returning to the stillness of your heart will bring about the absolute freedom of clarity.

Findlay McEwen

Chapter 6:

A Universal Heart

Chapter 6:

A Universal Heart

The state that the heart gives us access to is untouched by mental or emotional reverberations. It is free from all reverberation; it is simply still. This needs to be understood on a literal level: all physical, mental, emotional and spiritual experiences are reverberations. By learning to access the stillness of your heart, you begin to unfold into humanity's Common Ground. The reason I took a chapter to speak about society, then identity and finally emotions, is because these tend to be the stumbling blocks for many people when they attempt to enter the limitless space of their hearts. Mainly identity, and the emotions which follow, cause many of us to remain unaware of the beauty within the heart. When one learns to settle their heart, through steady awareness, they gain unrestricted access to the endless wealth of the Ultimate. Ever new and untouched, the state we are gifted access to through the heart is unlike anything you have experienced physically. The heart is a literal gateway out of suffering. However, it too comes with its hurdles and potholes if handled incorrectly. We must remain grounded and steady in our intellect and emotions to be able to hold and experience the heart in its unhindered brilliance. If you were thrown into the ocean without knowing how to swim and without a lifejacket, it could be tragic and it is no different than jumping into the heart. Yes, the space is available to us at any moment but we must do the correct preparatory work before we summersault off of the cliff. Now, I don't say these things to scare you but to have you realize the difference in experience when one can truly access the heart. If you had become accustomed to walking and that's all you knew, and the next thing you know you were thrown into the water to swim, it may cause you to panic and drown. Similarly, if all you knew was life as an individual with a limited identity, and the next thing you knew you were thrown into a silent ocean with no identity to claim, it could be very problematic. Really consider what that would be like to go from your experience of life now to one which is Universal with no individual 'I'. It's probably hard to imagine. That's why learning to hold your intellect and emotions at a steady distance is so important. As you begin your descent into the heart, you must be aware of what is your intellectual and emotional play versus your true self.

Many of you who have made it this far in the book may think that you have an intellectual understanding of our true nature: from stillness into reverberation and back into stillness. Another way to see it is from nothing into something and back into nothing. No matter how clear it may seem intellectually, if we are to move from intellectual understanding into absolute experience, we must prepare our foundations for the jump. That's why I have given time to dissect society, identity and emotions because they may be the hindrances you experience as you dive into your heart. That is also why I have given practical practices for you to do to help build the foundations required within body, mind and emotions. If you practice the exercises outlined throughout this book on a consistent basis, you will gradually begin to transition from an intellectual experience into an absolute experience.

What do I mean by absolute experience? Right now, your experience of life is mainly limited to your body, mind and emotions. For you to experience the stillness of your heart, you must transcend your body, mind and emotions. Your current experience of life is incomparable to the limitless nature of your heart. So, using your mind to intellectually understand what this book has said is one thing, but being able to unfold into that state intuitively is another. And that is another word I will emphasize when working with the heart, intuition. Working with the heart becomes intuitive once you are able to set your thoughts and emotions to the side. Once you are able to separate what is real and what is imagination; what is real and what are thoughts and emotions. As you begin to distinguish your true nature from the movement of the mind, you will notice how your intuition begins to take over. Life will become an intuitive process, rather than a mechanical reaction. Think about the way you go about life, most of it is mechanical. Most of it is predetermined by your habitual thinking and this is what I was getting at with identity. Based on your identity and the patterns it comes with, you live a mechanical life. That's where your heart comes in, it gives you the opportunity to know life intuitively and not mechanically. I feel like that is an important note to make, your heart is intuitive once you begin to identify thoughts and emotions. Noticing the intuitive nature of your own intellect is important as you begin to dive deeper into the realms of your heart. That same intuitive nature can guide your life forward and guide humanity forward if we begin to open to it on a larger scale. Earlier in the book I spoke about changing society, it is this intuitive nature which will help you transform society, one breath at a time. So, what do I mean when I refer to absolute experience? It is the experience of jumping into the heart intuitively.

As we transition into this absolute experience of the heart. Working with the Planet on a regular basis can play a vital role in facilitating that transition of experience. Making sure that your body is stable and connected to the Planet is very important, much like a tree blossoming into the sky. As the branches of your inner experience expand your roots must go deeper into the Planet. So that, when the winds of thought and emotions stir up, you can remain stable and strong in your clarity of experience. This is also why I emphasize consistent practice. If you truly want to know your true nature and go beyond the limited nature of your mind; if you sincerely wish to overcome your suffering, you must commit the time to transcend those experiences. As long as you are distracted by physical pleasures and pains, you will not go anywhere. That's why you must remain consistent as you go through the ups and downs of life to ensure that you are on a consistent track of expansion no matter how distracting life may become.

One final thing which I have failed to mention: as we accept life as an accumulation of different reverberations moving out from stillness, we will come to a place of equanimity. Where nothing is good or bad, right or wrong, mine or yours, this or that. A state where there is no room for judgement. Non-judgement could demand a chapter of its own, let alone a few sentences toward the end of the book but it is important to remember. To observe life like a scientist requires a lack of bias and a lack of judgement of yourself or others. Whatever you experience within, whatever you observe around you, do your best to remain within the neutral freedom of the heart. Judgement will entrap you within the experience you're judging, so do your best to simply watch it unfold. Life is simply moving as it needs to based on its tendencies and we are observing that movement. Once you become conscious of this, you rise above the bickering and confusion which seems to be engulfing the majority of Humanity at this point in time. That is how complex this mechanism of body is. We can wrap ourselves up in identity and emotions which then determine the way we act, think and feel, but little do we know everything we are claiming to be is a simple reverberation. Everything your enemy is, is simply a reverberation wrapped around the patterns of identity and emotion they hold. It can be built up into more with the help of our own thoughts and emotions but once we strip back physicality to its core, we see that all has come out of a simple reverberation. I say all this to have you really look at the life you are crafting and the beliefs you hold. Based on the surroundings you grew up in and the things you were subjected to your entire identity is moulded. It is this very identity which will go on to cause you, the holder, immense suffering throughout your lifetime. This is a shame because if you only knew how to hold your identity correctly, you would be able to use it for the betterment of all by acting as a neutral force amongst the ocean of Humanity's confusion.

Remember, your heart is a space which can transition your life from a limited individual experience into a Universal possibility. If you sit in your identity deeply rooted in the confines it imposes, you will not know freedom. If you spend your life building wealth or relationships, you will miss the whole point of being here. Every single one of you reading this does not have long left. In comparison to the age of this Planet or the Universe, your life is a blip. It means a lot to you when you're here but it means nothing on the grand scale of things. I don't say this to end the chapter on a sad point, I say it to have you take this to heart. Investigate your very life, where you have come from and where you will go. Don't just accept what you've been told from birth, don't settle for superficial belief. Find out for yourself. Is there really a gateway home which resides in the hearts of all conscious beings? Try the practices I have outlined and find out for yourself. Get outside and thank the planet for this experience. Don't let it slip through your fingers as you become distracted by the physical play unfolding around you. Enjoy it, yes, but don't accept it as the Ultimate. Open that car door and see what else there is to this experience. Your heart is the door and it's available to everyone, you just need the training to learn how to open it and jump out. I have outlined simple techniques to begin developing that steadiness required but if you want to jump into it fully with the 1:1 guidance, check out realizeone.org/call and book a free strategy call. We have developed a 12-week program to help anyone jump into their hearts and transition from the limited experience of their lives into a Universal one.

Findlay McEwen

Chapter 7:

Wind and Water

Chapter 7:

Wind and Water

Wind and water are two fundamental forces of this Creation which we can learn to work with as we dream in a brighter future. I will use this chapter to outline two simple ways we can utilize wind and water for our own mental and emotional benefit. As I wrote this book, I began by focusing on the Planet before I moved into our hearts but I would like to end with a focus on the Planet because, of course, it is the main character in Humanity's existence. So, how can we begin to work with wind and water for our mental and emotional benefit? I will outline two simple practices which I have found very beneficial for myself. These practices can be used anytime you encounter wind or a body of water. Beyond the mental and emotional benefits, they can provide us with a deeper, intuitive relationship with the Planet. As I mentioned, one of the key benefits of working with your heart is the intuitive development it fosters. As you become more aware of your heart, you may find that you become more receptive to the intuitive nature of your mind as well. These two practices can assist in that process.

Wind Resistance Practice:
1. Stand outside and feel the wind on your skin.
2. Settle your heart and close your eyes (closing your eyes is not necessary but can help with focus).

3. Feel the wind hit you and do your best to allow it to flow through you. Imagine it is flowing through every cell of your body.
4. In your heart, open in gratitude to the wind and invite it to remove any resistance you may be holding in your body, mind and emotions.
5. Allow it to move as it needs to, without anticipating its next move just observe the way it feels on your body.
6. Sit in this for as long as you feel comfortable and finish by thanking the wind for its assistance.

That is a simple yet profound way to utilize the movement of the wind while also developing an intuitive relationship with it. I have noticed in my own experience, that learning to work with nature intuitively will naturally teach us to step back from our thoughts and emotions. So, get out there in the wind and explore its movement.

The purpose of visualization is to use your intention to draw in a force which you wish to align with. This can be done when manifesting something you desire or when you're looking to work with a force greater than your own. These practices I have outlined in this book provide us with the opportunity to align and open up to forces which can help guide and balance us. With that in mind, I will outline the second practice which can prove very beneficial when dealing with emotional imbalance.

Water Cleansing Practice:
1. Find a body of water and place your attention on it.
2. Settle your heart and close your eyes (closing your eyes is not necessary but can help with focus).
3. Open yourself in gratitude to that body of water as your heart settles and your attention sharpens. This can be done by simply saying, "thank you" internally.

4. Use your internal gratitude to open yourself to that water and feel it balance your body. Sit in a space of grateful connection with that water.
5. Sit in this for as long as you feel comfortable and finish by thanking the water for its assistance.

Both of these practices are highly intuitive in nature. Learning to sit in your heart while projecting your intention forward is an intuitive skill which you will gradually learn if you put the practices of this book into action.

Common Ground

Findlay McEwen

Thunderbird Speaks

Oh, Thunderbird, your presence is precious.
You guide, protect and help all those who wish to reconnect with the land.
You are there when we need you, you are there when we don't.
Under your wings, I can carry any load.
Within your heart, I know exactly where to go.
Oh, Thunderbird, how lucky we are to have your platform.
May we use it for wisdom and guidance into inclusion.
Your intention is there for all to benefit from.
An intelligent force open to all.
Call on Thunderbird when you yearn for the Planet.
Call on Thunderbird when you need guidance which is organic.
Oh, Thunderbird, Oh Thunderbird!
Thank you!

Thunderbird is traditionally referred to within the stories of the First Peoples of the North Americas. I can only speak on my experience with its presence. The poem above is a reflection of my relationship with this intelligent force. Call on Thunderbird when you wish to reconnect with the land you are on or simply call on Thunderbird when you feel lost. The force we call Thunderbird will protect and light your way. As we move forward together as humanity, Thunderbird can play an important role in realigning our intentions back with the Planet these bodies have come from. It does not matter what country you are in or what ethnic background you have, Thunderbird will respond to those with a sincere call. Oh, Thunderbird!

Findlay McEwen

Conclusion

When we incarnate on a Planet, it is vitally important to understand the intention of that Planet, align with it and then find a way to best implement our own intention in alignment with the Planet. In regards to this Planet, if we can first make physical connection a priority, then learning to deepen our intuitive understanding will gently follow. In this book I have outlined various practices you can use to deepen your intuitive connection with the Planet. Learning to feel what it needs and then learning to translate that into thought form is a skill which requires training. As we go outside with the intention of listening to the Planet, we slowly build that understanding. Similar to what I mentioned earlier; as your relationship with this Planet deepens, you will be able to understand what it needs simply by being with it much like understanding the mental and emotional state of your friend, family member or partner, you will be able to translate the Planet's needs into your own form of understanding as you continue to develop your relationship with it. Your understanding of the Planet and your own intention will come in a way which is completely unique to you. Many people can have the same physical experience but experience it completely differently on a mental and emotional level, and your relationship with this Planet and your journey into your heart will be completely unique to you. The practices outlined in this book are pointers for you to develop your own unique relationship with this Planet while learning to settle into your heart.

Findlay McEwen

Join our 90-Day Inner Freedom Framework

If you are looking to put the words of this book into life-changing action, join our 90-Day Program which has been designed to transform your life by putting the principles and practices outlined in this book into a clear 12-week pathway. We will work with you over the course of those 12-weeks to ensure your inner transformation. If you would like to join our program, visit realizeone.org/call and book a free strategy call to get started.

Instagram: @findlaymcewen
Website: realizeone.org

Printed in Great Britain
by Amazon